THE WARRIOR'S HANDBOOK -

A GUIDE TO SPIRITUAL SURVIVAL

By hadassah

Autograph Page

Karyn,
My prayers & support are with you always!

Blessings,
Hadassah (Terri)

ACKNOWLEDGEMENTS

*I want to acknowledge my Messiah first and foremost and His Holy Spirt for the direction and guidance in my life. He sustained me over 40 years in **my desert** and I have never wanted. I had some close calls and some 11th hour things, but He never forsook me. He is a faithful God.*

I want to thank all the people who have touched my life to bring me to this moment, as I now realize that every chance meeting and every relationship was orchestrated by His loving hand. You know who you are, each and every one of you. I live and move and have my being in Him.

TABLE OF CONTENTS

INTRODUCTION

I was minding my own business as the story always goes and here's what happened...I was driving down I-95 in South Florida one sunny afternoon and I heard the Lord as clear as a bell speak in my spirit to write a book and He gave me the outline ever so quickly. I scrambled to find a pen and a scrap piece of paper to capture what it was I heard Him say. Interestingly, prior to that event, I had not been thinking of anything in particular but rather just driving along. Now there before me was the very rough draft of a book I knew I was purposed to write. I can only believe that as you hold this now, you are purposed to read this as well. That fateful day on I-95 happened over 10 years ago.

Initially I had the resolve and excitement of any new author as I began this journey. However as in any long journey, there are detours, road blocks, pot holes and unexpected turns. So went my life! I was quick to learn that the Sword of God cuts both ways and would impact me as well. I just had no idea to what extent. At one point in time, I had to lay the book down because in good conscience I could not complete it. I was falling into every pot hole and failing all the lessons I wanted to put forth. Thereafter, I endured a 10 year "Holy Spirit apprenticeship" and trial by fire. It became a long journey of examination and application for me and it was just what the doctor ordered. We all know the old adage "physician heal thyself"; and, we know that this is vitally important so as to be a vessel fit for use.

This was a time in my life that I was training in Haganah with an ex Israeli operative from the Golani Brigade. While learning these defensive tactics, I frequently found myself thinking about the parallels to the believer's walk and more specifically to spiritual warfare. Looking back on this literary journey, I've come to realize I wrote this book first and foremost for myself! I am now ready to bring this manuscript to you.

Blessings,
hadassah

SUMMARY

This book is about survival — survival at the highest and most strategic level — spiritual survival. Given the current political atmosphere, it is not uncommon to understand an assault, personally or nationally, as a very real possibility. Terrorists' threats and attacks are daily news items and a concern for all individuals. But, in addition to the tenuous world events, for followers of Messiah, there exists another imminent and foreboding danger on a minute to minute basis. It is the forces of the kingdom of darkness that are in battle against the believer. Defense against this danger is tantamount for our survival. The enemy of our souls wants to "take us out", to remove us from our tour of duty on planet earth. His desire is to trip us up in any way possible so as to distract, disable and prevent us from completing God's mission for us. The Word of God says that we are to be "sober minded and vigilant because our adversary, Satan walks about the earth like a roaring lion seeking whom he may devour"(1st Pet.5:8). Clearly, he is a real and present danger. For the believer, life is not a playground; it is a battlefield!

Have you been losing battles lately? Does the enemy keep ambushing you? Then, it is time for you to enroll in advanced spiritual warfare training. As soldiers in the army of the Lord, we need a thorough understanding of His training Manual. We also need to understand our enemy's objectives and tactics. Our Commander in Chief has made this information available to us. From the newest recruit to the most seasoned veteran, we can be victorious if we remain focused on His strategy and battle plan and not ours. Some soldiers have joined the ranks missing very basic training in this area which creates a liability for all involved.

Although this book is about intense spiritual warfare, it is NOT another book about casting out demons. On the other hand, don't be mistaken, though, because scripture does say that Jesus (Hebrew Yeshua) came to destroy the works of the devil (1st John 3:8), that He cast out demons and that we would do even greater works than these (John 14:12). But, there is a more important battle that is described in scripture. It says, that the "Kingdom of God suffers violence and the violent must take it by force (Matt.11:12).

There have been numerous books written about spiritual warfare and about putting on the "whole armor of God" (Eph. 6:10-17). This is not just good advice; it is an absolute necessity! Without the proper equipment for the battle, a soldier is of little use however brave he may be. But being a good soldier goes deeper than armor and equipment. It begins in the heart. Bringing the Kingdom of God to earth starts with warriors whose hearts are totally committed to their Commander in Chief. These particular warriors are the fighting elite. They strike fear in the heart of the enemy by their very presence on the battlefield.

Daily, the battlefields of life are littered with our own wounded and the walking dead…many taken out by "friendly fire"…by their own. In light of this, we desperately need to reexamine the Manual more thoroughly to be better prepared to "fight the good fight" (1st Tim.6:12). What is needed in this present time are soldiers who are fit for battle and who know who they are in Messiah, who understand the assignment, who know the enemy, and who know the terrain with all its minefields.

The impetus to write this book came from my 6 years of training in Haganah, the Israeli martial art of defense. "Defense" is the actual Hebrew translation of the word Haganah. Having been trained by an ex Golani Brigade operative, excellence was understood as the order of the day. The Golani Brigade is the Special Forces, an elite fighting unit of the Israel Defense Force (IDF).

Although a martial art setting like Haganah may seem to be an unlikely venue to recognize Godly principles, it was quickly apparent that the principles that were being taught were very applicable, not only to life in general, but to the spiritual aspect of life in particular. Haganah is unlike the various Eastern philosophies and martial art traditions with which most Americans are familiar. Eastern traditions of martial arts have a spiritual basis which is contrary to a Godly perspective. Haganah, on the other hand, arises from a military perspective and is, in fact, the military defense system of the world's most highly trained fighters in Israel.

Haganah has its roots deep in the Holy Land where the Jewish people lived under constant subjugation by foreign powers from early times. To deal with the constant conflicts with the various foreign powers, the Jews formed an underground army in 1919 known as the Haganah. The Haganah was a Jewish paramilitary organization comprised of mainly farmers whose role was to guard the Kibbutzim (settlements) and farms, to warn the residents of Arab attacks, and to repel the attackers. As time progressed, it became a much larger organization encompassing nearly all the youth and adults in the settlements as well as thousands of members from the cities. They acquired foreign arms and began to develop workshops to create hand grenades and simple military equipment. The Haganah went from being an untrained militia to a very capable army. This grassroots defense force became the first official Israeli

Special Forces known as Pal'mach, a Hebrew acronym for Plugot Machatz, which means, "strike platoon". The Pal'mach commandos received training called Kapap, an acronym for Krav Panim el Panim, or "face-to-face combat". In the U.S., this is referred to as "hand-to-hand combat."

Lotar was another tactic used by these Special Forces operators. Lotar directly translates to anti-terrorism warfare. Collectively, these defense forces ultimately became the distinguished Israeli Defense Force (IDF), Israel's current military force. The Haganah system that I was taught is the most effective combat and street fighting methodology of its time. There are two components to this system. The first is hand to hand combat training and the second is armed combat training including tactical knife fighting and combat shooting. The instructor continually updates and enhances the system as the IDF refines its techniques to better equip its fighting force.

Another important aspect of warfare in general and Haganah in particular is that it not only involves physical tactics of defense, but it employs a psychological stance, a particular mind set. This proves to be very valuable to the Haganah operative as intimidation is half the battle. A correct mind set is important to the believer as well, as we will see. To that end, I remember the instructor frequently telling us to fake it till we make it.

This formidable martial art, Haganah, a unique self-defense system integrating armed and unarmed combat techniques, is the basis of some of the principles and applications of this book. Because national warfare and spiritual warfare share similar principles, I will draw upon some of the principles of Haganah and apply them to our warfare as a believer.

In Haganah, we came in physically weak, and clueless as to the serious nature of the things that we were about to learn… principles that could possibly mean the difference between life and death for us. We were embarking on a journey to learn and more importantly internalize important principles for our survival. We learned: we are fighters; we will train well; we will learn to fight tired; we will train to keep our mind and our eyes on our objective; and we WILL conquer the enemy.

This is much like how we come into the Kingdom of God. We are spiritually weak and usually clueless as to the principles of the Kingdom and especially clueless to the rules of engagement that are needed for the battle that is suddenly upon us. We have the Manual in hand, the Bible, but, we need to learn how to effectively wield the Sword of the Spirit.

This book is established on the Word of God and on the Rock, Yeshua Ha Maschiach, (Hebrew Jesus the Messiah). It is from this vantage point that I will strive to understand the correct warrior's stance. This book will aid believers in the daily battles that are waged against their souls. It will inform, encourage and undergird them as they "fight the good fight" (1Tim.6:12). Awareness of the enemy's tactics and implementation of God's resources can minimize potential battle scars and ensure a victorious battle. This book is a call to arms! It is a call to return to the Word of God and to bring the Kingdom of God to earth. This book is written for every believer that is enlisted to battle and for the countless many already lying wounded and dying in the trenches. "Blessed be the Lord my strength which teacheth my hands to war, and my fingers to fight" (Ps. 144:1)!

Chapter I

OUR IDENTITY

The Bible often uses military metaphors and in fact, the Apostle Paul likened the believer's experience to being in the army of the Lord. It is a necessity to be properly equipped and trained during our tour of duty on planet earth. Not only is it important to learn the physical aspects of defense, it is of utmost importance to have and maintain a proper psychological mindset. That proper psychological mindset is to be an integral part of your identity which will ensure a victorious outcome. Even more fundamental though is the fact that there must be a realization that there IS a war being waged. Ignorance of the enemy and of warfare will not keep you out of the battle. On the contrary, it makes you extremely vulnerable. Believers frequently live a life of defeat because they don't know or they fail to understand the nature of their position and the necessary effective strategies of spiritual warfare. When they said yes to God, they entered into a war with the devil himself. They frequently don't realize that they are on the front lines.

God, Himself, through the apostle Paul writing Ephesians, reminds us of this battle and of an enemy that wants to wrestle us to the ground and render us ineffective for the Kingdom of God. The word translated wrestle in Ephesians 6:12 speaks of a "hand-to-hand fight"...a fight characterized by trickery, cunningness and strategy. Because of the nature of the enemy and the serious nature of the conflicts, it is imperative that we have accurate combat intelligence on our enemy. That intelligence can be found in the ultimate Manual, the Word of God.

The book of Ephesians is a book that speaks to aspects of warfare. In addressing warfare, it emphasizes the believer's relationship to the principalities and powers behind it.

Ephesians 2:20-22 reminds us that we are above Satan's principalities and powers. They are not above us, oppressing us and controlling our destinies with their diabolical activities. We are above them! Armed with this information, we can pray with confidence and authority and know that we can take back what the enemy has robbed (Mark11:23-24.) We can effectively war in the heavens so that the Kingdom of God is established and promoted on earth (Matt.11:12). Ephesians 6:11 tells us to "put on the whole armor of God, that we may be able to stand against the wiles of the devil", the cunning devices, the crafty deceit, and the constant battering. As we do this, we must understand our spiritual DNA…what we are made of. It is in the early chapters of Ephesians that it outlines who we are in Messiah while it "fleshes out" these positional truths in the daily arena of life.

First and foremost, God wants us to know who we are; and then, what we are called to do. As important as our identity may be though, we can never fully understand who WE are until we fully understand who HE is! He created the universe (Gen 1:1); He is the GREAT I AM (Ex. 3:14)! He forgives all our iniquities; He heals all our diseases; He redeems our life from destruction; He crowns us with loving kindness and tender mercies; He satisfies our mouth with good things so that our youth is renewed; He executes righteousness and judgment for us when we are oppressed; He is merciful and gracious, slow to anger and plenteous in mercy (Ps. 103:3-8). He knew us before we were in our mother's womb (Ps. 139). He knows us intimately. He knows about all of our tears, the number of hairs on our head and He holds our days in His hands (Ps. 56:8, Luke 12:7, Ps. 31:15). He binds up the wounds of the broken hearted (Ps. 147:3) and He comes to SET THE CAPTIVES FREE (Is. 61:1-3) that HE MIGHT BE GLORIFIED! As He has set us free, we too are called to set others free by His grace by sharing that very same good news! The Kingdom of God has come! The Lord is our Salvation!! The Lord is our Rock, our Strength, our Fortress, and our Deliverer. He is our Shield and our Stronghold (Ps. 18:2). He is a shield to all who trust in Him (Ps. 18:30). He is our ever present help in time of need (Ps. 46:1). He is the Glory and the Lifter of our head (Ps. 3:1-3). He is the Aleph and the Tav (the first and last letters of the Hebrew alphabet) meaning He is the beginning and the end (Rev. 1:8, Rev. 22:13). He calls us to war!

To really know about God and who He is; however, we must also seek to understand His character. Only in studying the names of God, can we learn more about our Commander in Chief and how He dealt with His soldiers in the past. Names in the Bible were often an indication of a person's character or some particular quality of their character. The Old Testament contains a number of names for God which reveal Him in some aspect of His character and dealings with man. We will look at a few of these names.

Elohim is the first name mentioned in Genesis and is translated God. It is mentioned approximately 32 times. Elohim is said to be derived from the shorter El which means mighty, strong or prominent. This word El itself is translated God over 250 times and is frequently connected with circumstances which would invoke the great power of God. In Numbers, for instance, it is the name El (Hebrew God) that is used to speak about the One who brought the Israelites out of Egypt. In Deuteronomy 10:17, it is this word El which is used to relay the One who is "great, mighty, and dreadful" and it is the word El which is used in the name Almighty God. The name Elohim as it is used alone in Gen 1:1 to 2:4 conveys the idea of creative governing power and of omnipotence and sovereignty. An interesting peculiarity about the word Elohim is that it is in the plural. Most Christian scholars regard this plurality as reference to the Godhead being understood also as the Trinity, the triune nature of God. Among many other similar references, in Gen. 1:26, Elohim even speaks of Himself as Us when He says, "let Us make man in Our image". There is solace in this great name of God signifying supreme power, sovereignty, and glory on one hand and covenant relationship which He forever keeps, on the other hand. Thus, He says, "I will be to you a God (Hebrew Elohim) and you shall be my people" (Ex. 6:7, Lev. 26:12, Jer. 7:23, Jer. 11:4, Jer.24:7, Jer. 30:22, Jer. 30:22, Jer. 31:33, Ez. 11:20, Ez. 14:11, Ez. 36:28, Ez. 37:23, Ez. 37:27, Hosea 2:23, Zech. 8:8, Zech. 13:9). Elohim reminds us that He is faithful and keeps His word. In Deuteronomy 7:9, it says, "Know therefore that the Lord your God is a faithful God, keeping His covenant of love to a thousand generations of those who love Him and keep His commandments". His covenant is an everlasting covenant (Gen. 17:7, Ezek. 37:26). Moreover, He adds, "I will be with you till the end of time" (Matt. 28:20).

After the name Elohim, the name Jehovah appears or the combination Elohim-Jehovah. The name Jehovah is translated Lord and reveals God as a Supreme Being of moral and spiritual attributes, love, justice, righteousness and holiness (Gen 2:4, Lev. 19:2, Lev. 24:16, Ps. 11:7, Dan. 9:14, Gen. 18:25, Jer. 31:3, Isa. 45:22, 24, Ps. 89:15-16). It is as Jehovah that He manifests Himself in covenants and acts of deliverance and redemption. To the children of Israel he says, "I am Jehovah. I will bring you out" (Ex. 6:6). In Exodus 34:5-7, we see Jehovah, a God who is merciful and gracious, slow to anger, and abundant in loving kindness, forgiving transgressions and sins.

Gen.17:1-2 reveals God Almighty (El Shaddai). Shaddai primarily means "breasted" (shad Hebrew breast) and it indicates the powerful, all bountifulness of God. When this is connected with the word El, it confirms that He is the One mighty to nourish, supply and satisfy. As He reveals Himself to Abraham as the El Shaddai who is mighty in sufficiency and willing to dispense of His bounty, it is clear that He imparts fullness and fruitfulness to all who trust in Him and wait upon Him (Gen. 11:11). El Shaddai speaks to the mothering, nurturing aspects of the God who has inexhaustible stores of grace and unending love poured out for us. Scripture tells us that, "His mercies are new each day" (Lamentations 3:22-23). El Shaddai is our Father with might and strength and He is our mother with bountiful provisions.

There are also many compounded names of God that arise out of historical events. These compounded names portray some aspect of the character of God as meeting human need. The name Jehovah Jireh is one such name. A most significant Biblical example of this is found in Genesis 22. It involves the story of Abraham on the mountain about to obediently sacrifice his only son, a prototype of what God Himself was prepared to offer. Isaac, his son, sees the wood and the fire but then asks his father where the lamb was for the offering. Abraham's answer to this was that God will provide Himself a lamb for the offering. Abraham called the name of that place, Jehovah Jireh (Gen.22:14) because we know that God ultimately did provide a lamb that was caught in a nearby thicket for the sacrifice. So, we understand the translation of this name as, God will provide.

The name Jehovah Rophe means God heals. In Exodus 15, we are told about God supplying water for the Israelites as they crossed the desert on the way to the Promised Land. It goes on to say, in verse 26, that God said if the Israelites "harkened to His voice" and "did what is right in His sight", He would not bring any diseases upon them. He stated, "I am Jehovah that heals thee". He intimately cares about us and all aspects of our life as the God of restoration and healing.

Although there are several other names of God, Jehovah Nissi is an important name to consider when talking about warfare. It means Jehovah, my banner (Ex. 17:15). We are reminded of the story of Moses holding up the rod, the God given rod, as the children of Israel battled the Amalekites at Rephidim. This was the same wonder working rod which brought the plagues upon Egypt and which opened the Red Sea for the deliverance of the children of Israel. It was the rod symbolizing the mighty hand and outstretched arm of the Lord, the rod of God. When Moses held up the rod, the Israelites prevailed and when he lowered it, the enemy prevailed. It was this rod, as the banner of God, which brought the victory. It was there at Rephidim that God revealed Himself as Jehovah Nissi, the Lord my banner. Israel's warring soldiers were quick to learn that to God alone belonged the victory! That rod was a symbol of His presence, power and capability.

In ancient times, a banner was not like a flag as we know it today. Often it was a pole with a shiny ornament attached to it which glittered in the sun. Although there are several meanings for the word, banner, here the meaning used is to glisten. It is also translated pole, ensign or standard. The Hebrew word for standard is nos-sah, a primary root associated with the Hebrew word nes (miracle). The word nes also carries the meaning of something elevated or lifted up as a pole or banner. It was a signal for God's people to rally to Him and to His cause, His battle.

It was the rod of Elohim held aloft in Moses' upraised hands as God's banner over them and the light of His countenance upon them that were Israel's victory. Israel's battles are analogous to our own present day battles and spiritual warfare. The Amalekites were the first enemy to appear to the redeemed people of Israel. In Exodus 17:16, we read, "Jehovah hath sworn that Jehovah will have war with Amalek from generation to generation." This scripture is relevant today because it is a prototype of the present world which lies in wickedness (1st John 5:19) and can represent the current forces of darkness that stand opposed to God. The characteristics are the lust of the flesh, the lust of the eyes, and the pride of life (1st John 2:16) which represent the roots of our own battles. As soldiers of the Lord, we are warned about the constant internal battle (Gal. 5:17) where our flesh and the Spirit within are contrary to one another and are constantly warring. Just like the Israelites, we must raise up Jehovah Nissi, the Lord our banner (Ex. 17:15) to ensure our ongoing victory. He is the banner over our warfare. He is our covering. Remember that Isaiah 59:19 tells us that, "…when the enemy comes in like a flood, the Spirit of the Lord will lift up a standard against him." He conquered before us. John 16:33 tells us that we will have tribulations in this world but that He has overcome the world. Faith in this assures our victory because we are told that "this is the victory that overcomes the world, EVEN OUR FAITH" (1st John 5:4). We are to be strong in the Lord and in the power of His might. We can go from strength to strength with each victory and know that we always triumph in Messiah (2nd Cor. 2:14). After all, if God be for us, who can be against us (Rom. 8:31)?

And, finally, who could forget the story of young David in 1st Samuel chapter 17? We are told that the young lad, David, came to the giant Goliath and said to him, "…thou comest to me with a sword, and with a spear and with a shield: but I come to thee in the name of the Lord of Hosts (Hebrew Jehovah Sabaoth), the God of the armies of Israel, whom thou hast defied" (1st Sam. 17:45). Obviously, David had a Divine revelation of the nature and character of God to be without equal weapons and to make such a bold statement.

This name of God, Jehovah Sabaoth (Hebrew Lord of Hosts), is the most used compound name of God appearing about 270 times in the Tenach (Old Covenant). We see it in the writings found in 1st Samuel, Isaiah, Jeremiah, Amos, Zechariah, Malachi and Psalms to name a few. It says several things about the nature of God but mostly it emphasizes God's ultimate power over the whole universe and over every living thing. The image that comes to mind with this title is a mighty military Commander who with the wink of an eye can summon rank upon rank of protective power. What a Commander in Chief we have! And finally, He is and always will be Jehovah Tsidkenu (Hebrew the Lord our Righteousness)!

This brief summary only gives us a limited understanding of who our Commander in Chief is, but still, it is incumbent upon us to make particular note of the scriptural injunction that says, "...AS HE IS SO ARE WE in this world" (1st John 4:17).

More details about our specific identity are given in the first three chapters of Ephesians. Not only does God tell us who we are in Messiah, but, in the last three chapters, He instructs us to walk in the light of who we are. In Ephesians, we are told that we were chosen in Him before the foundation of the world (Eph. 1:4). Moreover, it goes on to say that He predestined us to adoption to Himself through Jesus, the Messiah (Eph. 1:5) and that in Him we are redeemed through His blood. The apostle Paul reminds us that God has made known to us the mystery of His will and that we have an inheritance having been predestined according to His purpose. And, finally, the Scripture tells us that we are sealed in Him with the Holy Spirit of promise (Eph. 1:7-13). In case that wasn't enough, we are told that we are seated in heavenly places in Messiah Jesus ABOVE principalities and powers (Eph. 2:6, Eph. 2:20-22). As we proceed, we will understand just how important that particular vantage point is in reference to warfare.

By now, you might be thinking, "Why ME?" "Why choose ME?" His response to that would be that salvation is His gift to you. We are all saved by His grace. We are His "workmanship" created for good works which God prepared beforehand (Eph. 2: 8-10). We are no longer strangers or aliens but we are now a part of God's household (Eph. 2:19), being called out of darkness into His marvelous light (1st Pet. 2:9). We are also called the sons of God (1st John 3:1). We are called to walk in authority and to take dominion (Gen. 1:26-28, Gen. 2:15) because He has a specific plan for each of us (Jer. 29:11). We are called to "show forth the praises of God" who has called us out of darkness (1st Pet. 2:9). And finally, "The Lord your God has chosen you out of all the peoples on the face of the earth to be…his treasured possession" (Deut. 7:6, Deut. 14:2).

Obviously, the Lord thinks we are capable of receiving and walking in this destiny because He CHOSE us! Remember, we didn't choose Him; He chose us! He selected you and me and drafted us into His army, His select group! It has been said that man is defined in relationship. There is no greater relationship than one forged between man and his Maker. It is in that relationship that we are given purpose and direction (Jer. 29:11, Ps. 139). We are earmarked for service and carry the favor of God as we walk in His ways. It is through our service, our tour of duty, our unique calling that many are snatched out of darkness and are brought into the Kingdom that He might be glorified.

God has placed eternity in our hearts (Eccles. 3:11) and has given us dreams and callings that match our unique God given DNA. These dreams and callings constitute our assignment, our tour of duty. Our dreams and callings wake us up to God's purpose in our life. They bring us together with those who are of a similar dream or calling; they connect us with others. We can look at the life of Joseph for an interesting glimpse of God's divine workings in matters like this. Scripture says that Joseph had the favor of God upon him. Then it says he drove a nice Mercedes and lived in a mansion, right? No!! It says that he was thrown into prison! The favor of God was upon him and yet he was thrown into prison. I'm sure as you are reading this, there are many who can relate to a similar situation in their own life…maybe not exactly a prison but a similar uncomfortable situation in which they found themselves. I know I can relate. Frequently, things like this can cause us to initially question God's love for us because we don't see the total picture. And, during those times, the enemy would love to capitalize on those situations and whisper in our ear that we have been forsaken and forgotten and left for dead in the trenches. He would love for us to believe that we are in every foxhole alone! Let's not believe that for a minute because just as He did not forget Joseph, he has not forgotten us! Getting back to Joseph, we see that his calling and his God given destiny were being worked out in this dire situation. Joseph's dream and calling brought him in contact with Pharaoh and away from his brothers. In contact with the person who would help him achieve the plans of God…even unknowingly. That's how God sometimes works in our lives. Through unexpected changes and circumstances,

He draws us to the people and places He wants us to transform for Him. Our dreams and callings all serve to dispel the darkness and the deception of the enemy in our minds about who we are and why we were commissioned into this man's army in the first place (Eph. 1:4, Eph. 1:11). When we only see all the problems facing us, we need to remember that our calling and destiny rests upon the sovereignty of God, not upon us because nothing can thwart the plans of God (Job 42:2, Is. 14:27). During our tour of duty, God redeems and uses our past sufferings and mistakes for His glory and to minister to others, if we allow it. If we do not allow God to redeem our past, we can become bitter instead of being an agent of healing for someone else. We may think that our past mistakes disqualify us for service, when, in fact, they position us to be highly trained warriors in His service. Joseph was weak and powerless in prison but ultimately was able to minister to those who were as weak and powerless as he once was. When we completely walk out our tour of duty, the fullness of our gifts and talents are realized and we are able to reach others and glorify God! Our tests and battles in life qualify us to be in the Special Ops, so to speak. Because we have our battle scars, unbelievers can trust that we can speak to their hurts and disappointments as one who "knows". Frequently God has your path cross with that particular person to whom only you with your particular set of scars could minister. That's what being redeemed is all about.

Most importantly in this tour of duty, we are called to be good soldiers for Jesus and to endure tough times as warriors (2nd Tim 2:3-4.) In the Scriptures, we have quite a few examples of warriors, but none stands out more than David. In Psalm 144:1-15, we hear the prayer of this skilled warrior. From his days as a shepherd boy and throughout his reign as king of the nation of Israel, God empowered him in the art of strategic prayer and warfare. David's skill and expertise were gleaned in the midst of a variety of battles ranging from encounters with bears and lions to his confrontation with Goliath, and to the battle he fought with Absalom, whose defiant insurrection almost cost him his kingdom. God, in His sovereignty, allowed David to learn about warfare in the MIDST of the battle. In Psalm 144, David lets us know that it was Jehovah Gibbor, the Mighty Man of War who taught him the strategies and tactics needed and who provided the divine empowerment for success. Because we know that all scripture is given for our example and teaching (2nd Tim. 3:16-17, 1st Cor.10:11), we can learn an important lesson from David's situation.

First of all, we see that one of the ways we can become skillful warriors is to be trained and placed in the MIDST of the battle. Unlike Haganah, where we practice the military combatives over and over to establish "muscle memory", in the arena of spiritual warfare, practice does not make perfect. Perfect practice makes perfect. As spiritual warriors, we can never get the level of training we need in order to become effective by engaging in "war games" like Haganah. We must face a real enemy on a real battlefield. Then and only then can we gain true experience and come forth as gold tried in the fire (Rev. 3:18). We frequently find ourselves learning by failing. Simply reading the Bible or attending church or seminars on spiritual warfare will never make us an effective warrior. Proverbs implies that knowledge without experience is folly. Taking the wisdom from the warriors who walked before us can help us learn to war more effectively.

Although Moses is not necessarily known primarily as a warrior, scripture does provide some graphic descriptions of his military conquest and the subsequent decimation of the various tribes that occupied Canaan and its surrounding areas (Deut. 20:17, Num. 21:2-3, Deut. 2:24, Deut. 2:31-35, Deut. 3:3-6, Deut. 20:16-17, Num. 25:17). God ordered the Israelites under the leadership of Moses to exterminate all the inhabitants of Canaan and to take their land and not to "...leave anything alive that breathes" (Deut. 20:16-17). Moses and the Israelites successfully conquered these surrounding tribes in preparation to possess the Promised Land that the Lord gave them as an inheritance. Moses was obedient to the commands of the Lord. But, for various complicated reasons, he never entered the Promised Land. Many believe Moses was not allowed to enter the Promised Land because of the "rock" incident detailed in Numbers 20. However, his fall from grace may have started much earlier. When Moses was up on the mountain top with God receiving the Law, the people got tired of waiting and they made a golden calf after the lust of their flesh (Exodus 20: 7-9). When God spoke to Moses and said He was going to destroy the people for their idolatry, Moses asked that God spare them. Essentially, Moses was asking God to save the people from Himself. Moses failed to understand that God is righteous and just and needed to purge this sin from His people and purify them through judgment. In the ensuing chapters, we see that God was not pleased. In Exodus 32:34, The Lord tells Moses that He spared the people for now, so to speak, but would address their sin in the day of His visitation. God was saying in essence that the present generation was perverse and needed to be destroyed to allow the next generation to receive the mantle of Moses. God offered a new generation to come out of Moses, but he refused the offer and instead chose to plead for and "save" the wicked generation from God's wrath. However, scripture reminds us that God's judgments are inevitable (1st Pet. 4:17). Moses ultimately lost his patience with his charges and it eventually led to the incident in Numbers 20 where he was barred from the Promised Land. Numbers 20:12 also tells us that Moses' sin was unbelief. Subsequently, Moses was instructed by God to commission Joshua and "...strengthen him for he will lead this people across and will cause them to inherit the land that you see" (Deut. 3:28). Moses was a warrior and a servant of God but his unbelief, his disobedience and his decision regarding the judgment of sin proved to be very costly for him. Obedience is important for a warrior, and it is equally as important to have the heartbeat of God in all matters. As scripture demonstrated in Exodus 20, humanistic viewpoints and sympathies rarely align with God's viewpoint on life's issues.

Moses led the Israelites out of Egypt and Joshua, the next warrior on the scene, led them into the Promised Land.

Joshua had a different perspective on the judgment of sin. After losing a battle at Ai, God pointed out to Joshua that the people had disobeyed Him. Joshua was quick to seek out the sin in the camp and to correct it. Achan had brought the sin and judgment upon the camp by keeping a portion of the spoils from their conquests and hid them in his tent when he was commanded not to do so by God, Himself. When it was discovered, Joshua and the people of Israel stoned Achan and his whole family (Josh. 7:10-26). The Israelites learned the hard way that what one person does could affect the well-being of the whole nation.

Both Joshua and the people who fought alongside him had God's zeal for justice and judgment, unlike the previous rebellious, complaining generation. Not only did Joshua possess God's zeal for justice and judgment, he had a warrior's DNA. In Exodus 32:15-18, it is recorded that when Joshua and Moses were descending the mountain, they heard noise coming from the camp below. Joshua thought the noise he heard was "...a noise of war in the camp" while Moses thought it was "the people singing". As it is recorded, the Lord wanted us to note how Joshua was "war-oriented". The spirit in him was always ready to do battle with the enemy. He knew there was land to conquer and kingdoms to be taken. That is why he was so willing to fight the giants in the Promised Land despite the other spies' bad report (Numbers 14:6-10). There was not a bone of spiritual lethargy in Joshua. But, those who did not share Joshua's spirit wanted to stone him and Caleb.

Joshua's most memorable victory came at Jericho. He was obedient to the Lord's directives to march around the walls 6 times during the 6 days and then 7 times during the 7th day (Josh. 6). Joshua knew about war and taking cities; and, in this situation, he also understood that a spiritual battle was being waged as well. The Lord instructed Joshua that this battle had to be won through the priests with the Ark of the Covenant. The ark speaks to being exposed to God's face and His face brings death to anything earthly or ungodly. As warriors fighting in the spirit of Joshua, it is imperative that we come "panim el panim" (Hebrew face to face) with our God and that we also relinquish faith in all earthly methods as we learn to "rest" in the Lord. God, Himself, tells us to strive to enter into that rest (Heb. 4:1-3, Heb. 4:11). Chapters 3 and 4 of the book of Hebrews give us insight into the failure of the Israelites to enter into His rest as they were instructed. Hebrews 3:19 states, "So we see that they could not enter in because of UNBELIEF". Chapter 4 also warns US of the present danger of unbelief. For the Israelites, it was belief about the Promised Land, but for us now who have already believed for Salvation (Jesus, Hebrew Yeshua, Salvation, God saves), it is about CONTINUING FAITH in His eternal promises and His ability to "perfect that which concerns us" (Ps. 138:8). We need to rest in the faith and belief that the One who started the good work in us will finish it until the day of His return (Phil. 1:6).

David understood rest. He reminds us in Psalm 37:7-9: "Rest in the Lord, and wait patiently for Him, fret not thyself because of him who prospers in his way, because of the man who brings wicked devices to pass. Cease from anger and forsake wrath, fret not thyself in any way to do evil. For evil doers shall be cut off; but those that wait upon the Lord, they shall inherit the earth."

Rest is one of the greatest gifts God gave to mankind (Lev. 23:1-3). The Hebrew word for rest is nuach...to rest, to be quiet. It is synonymous with Shabbat...to cease or to rest. Rest is more than mere inactivity. It is resting in God and in His finished work. The rest of God is not a rest from work, but in work; not the rest of inactivity, but of the harmonious working of all the faculties and affections of will, heart, imagination, and conscience because each has found in God their ideal fulfillment and satisfaction. It is necessary for us to cease from our own works and schemes trying to exact our own way and to allow the Ruach Ha Kodesh (Hebrew Holy Spirit) to live through us so we may walk out our destiny (Heb. 4:9-11), our divine tour of duty. It is only then that the battle to be holy stops. For the believer, rest is only doing what the Father does and only saying what the Father says. Grace works when we rest (Deut. 6:10-11). In Psalm 91, the Hebrew word used for dwells is yashab which means to sit down, to be set, to remain, to abide, implying to rest under the shadow of the Almighty.

Rest was so important in God's agenda that when He instituted the Feasts (Lev. 23), the Sabbath rest was the first feast

He ordained (Lev. 23:1-3). He said we are to keep these Feasts forever throughout our generations (Lev. 23:14, 21, 31, 41). He added, "They are the Feasts of the Lord", not of Israel, not of the Jews, but of the Lord. There is nowhere in Scripture where we are told to discontinue celebrating the Feasts of the Lord because they were meant to be foreshadows of Messiah. Each Feast represents the being and work of Messiah who would come. Each time we celebrate the Feasts and Holy Days, we acknowledge the work of Messiah. It has been said that the Old Covenant is eighty percent the New Covenant concealed and the New Covenant is eighty percent the Old Covenant revealed. The first Covenant gave us the prophecies foreshadowing the Messiah; the second Covenant was the renewal and fulfillment of those prophecies in Messiah. He is our Rest. Shabbat (Hebrew Sabbath, rest) is the first (primary) Feast of the Lord that we are told to keep.

In Mark 2:27-28, we are again reminded that the Sabbath rest was created for man not for God. In addition, it is our time to remember and honor the first and great commandment. That commandment is to love God with all of our heart, mind and strength. As we rest and reflect and give thanks, we gain a deep and profound understanding that sums up our existence on planet earth and that allows us to live in peace despite our often distressing circumstances. We can live in this understanding because we are told, "we know that ALL things work together for good to them that love God, to them who are the called according to His purpose" (Rom. 8:28-29) as we are conformed into His image. He will finish the good work that He has started in us and He will perfect that which concerns us (Phil. 1:6, Ps. 138:8) through the work of His Spirit (Hebrew His Ruach) in our lives.

Rest begins in the mind. The place where Satan (Hebrew Ha Satan) launches attacks at you is in your mind, in your imagination. 3rd John 2 tells us that we are to prosper in all things even as our soul prospers. Our soul is our will, mind and emotions. Our emotions follow closely on the heels of our thinking and often are flags that something is wrong in our thinking. That is why it is vitally important to "renew your mind daily by the washing in the Word" (Rom. 12:2; Titus 2; Ps. 51). It helps us rest easier when we remember that God is sovereign and He is in control of everything. King David so powerfully summed it up in the following scripture: "Yours, O lord, is the greatness, and the power, and the glory, and the victory, and the majesty: for all that is in the heaven and in the earth is yours; yours is the kingdom, O Lord and You are exalted as head above all. Both riches and honor come of you, and you reign over all; and in your hand is power and might; and in your hand it is to make great, and to give strength unto all" (1st Chron. 29:11).

As we are being conformed with the daily washing of the Word, we must be willing to die to self, crucify our flesh (our way of thinking) and be resurrected in God's glorious countenance (Heb. 4:1-11). We are to manifest a strong-willed warrior nature that is capable of pulling down spiritual strongholds all the while recognizing our human weaknesses before God and "resting" in His strength to perform through His Word. As a warrior in His service, it is of utmost importance to be filled with His Spirit, to have His heartbeat, to be obedient, and to be quick to judge the sin in our camp and to correct it. David walked in might; Moses walked in the Glory; Joshua walked in faith; we are called to walk in faith AND in the Spirit in these last days of the battle.

And finally, there is one unlikely warrior we should look at as we seek to understand God's viewpoint. That is Gideon whose story is told in Judges 6-8. He may have been voted least likely warrior if they were doing a survey that day.

Israel had fallen into sin and idolatry and God PERMITTED the Midianites to invade the land each year and rob the harvest. One day, Gideon was hiding out in the winepress threshing wheat so the Midianites wouldn't find it. God sought him out by sending an Angel to announce to him, "The Lord is with you, you mighty man of valor (Judges 6:12)"! This was in direct opposition to how Gideon saw himself. Gideon saw himself as young and weak and ineffective. This an important point because how we view ourselves definitely affects the way we engage in warfare. We must have God's viewpoint of who He says we are. God saw Gideon as a "...mighty man of valor."

The Lord commissioned Gideon to lead Israel in battle against the Midianites. I'm sure that was the last thing that Gideon wanted to do; but, he was obedient to God's directive. However, there was one small problem. Gideon was sorely outnumbered more than four to one. There were 135,000 Midianties to Gideon's 32,000 men. Imagine Gideon's surprise when God told him that his numbers were too great (Judges 7:12)! The Lord told him to send the men home who were afraid and 22,000 departed. Gideon was left with 10,000 men. He was now outnumbered more than thirteen to one but God was not finished yet. To Gideon's astonishment, He said, "The people are still too many (Judg. 7:4)." God had another test for those men who were to remain. They had to go down to the river to drink. Only those men that lapped water like a dog passed the test (Judg. 7:4-7). They were the men that proved to be vigilant as they drank the water while on one knee with their shields on their other arm. When Gideon and his men finally faced their adversaries, they were outnumbered 450 to one. There was a total defeat of the Midianites demonstrating that God's ways are far from our ways (Is. 55:8-9). For God, the question is not "how many people?" but "what kind of people?"

In God's army, we cannot give way to fear and run. We cannot bury our faces in the affairs of life and forget that we are in a spiritual conflict with unseen forces of darkness who are always watching to catch us unprepared. This warfare that we are fighting requires unceasing vigilance in every situation and demands conscious, personal discipline. We are warned, "Be sober, be vigilant; because your adversary the devil walks about like a roaring lion, seeking whom he may devour" (1st Pet. 5:8). To ignore the warning is to be vulnerable to subtle, unpredictable but assured assaults of Satan. Warriors must develop their character as they go from victory to victory and advance against the enemy. As gold is tried in the fire (Job 23:1, 1st Pet. 4:12, Rev. 3:18-19), character is developed in the trials and battles of life. Character is the key to walking in your destiny and fulfilling your personal tour of duty. It is also one of the essential elements of spiritual warfare. If the enemy can continually wound you and keep you on the sidelines of life, he has successfully rendered you ineffective. Trials and tribulations are frequently the tools God uses to build character traits in us. In Romans 5:3-4, we see that trials produce perseverance and trials produce patience which equals waiting with contentment! Endurance (perseverance) is needed to survive the spiritual battles we face. So, perseverance is fighting the battle while you wait with contentment. Perseverance produces character. Character produces hope and hope produces appointments preordained by God. Joseph's prison test was one of his tests of character. Character occurs when what you believe infiltrates your behavior. James reminds us that "...the testing of our faith produces patience" (and endurance) and that we "...must let patience (and endurance) have its perfect work" (James 1:2-4). In other words, we must continue to endure until God's purpose has been fully worked out and He brings that particular aspect of the trial to an end. Then, we will be on to the next battle assignment!

Chapter II

OUR ASSIGNMENT AND PREPARATION

The objective of this war is to make known to all that cross our paths the good news of the Kingdom and to set as many captives free as possible. The number one priority for us during our tour of duty is to "...seek first His Kingdom..." In the passage of Isaiah 61:1-3, we are introduced to the King who will rule in the glorious Kingdom Isaiah has just described. Jesus (Hebrew Yeshua) read from this passage in the synagogue (see Luke 4:17-21) and said, "This day is this scripture fulfilled in your ears". The Lord was sent to preach the good news of the Kingdom, to bind up the broken hearted, to proclaim liberty to the captives, to open the prison to those who are bound, to proclaim the acceptable year of the Lord and to comfort all who mourn. He gives beauty for ashes, the oil of joy for mourning, and the garment of praise for the spirit of heaviness that He might be glorified (Is. 61:1-3). Yeshua brought the message of freedom, restoration and reconciliation to a dying world and that is exactly what WE are called to do!

All of these tasks comprise the basic assignment for all soldiers. Then, there are specific directives given individually as the Spirit speaks and leads which constitutes that individual's personal tour of duty. Through the instructions in the Manual, the Word of God we are told that we are to have compassion on some (Jude 1:22), snatch some from hell fire (Jude 1:23), reprove, rebuke and exhort some (2nd Tim. 4:2, Heb. 3:13), weep with those who weep (Rom. 12:15), comfort all who mourn (Is. 61:3), feed those around us with His Word (1st Pet. 5:2), and keep pressing on toward the mark of the prize of the high calling (Phil. 3:14). But, most importantly we are to be ready to preach the Word in season and out (1st Tim. 4:2) and to "...declare His glory among all the nations and His wonders among all the people" (Ps. 96:3). We are to let our light so shine that others will see our good works and will glorify God (Matt. 5:16). Moreover, we are told in Matthew by our Commander in Chief to "...go to the lost sheep of the house of Israel, and as ye go, preach, saying, the Kingdom of Heaven is at hand. Heal the sick, cleanse the lepers, raise the dead, cast out devils: freely ye have received, freely give" (Matt. 10:5-10).

In Romans 12:1-12, Paul tells us to present our bodies as a living sacrifice holy and acceptable to God which is our reasonable service. He goes on to describe several things that are the perfect will of God for us such as not being conformed to the world, renewing our mind, being humble, being kindly predisposed to one another, rejoicing in hope, being patient in tribulation and continuing in prayer. Romans 12:18 reminds us that as much as is possible within us to live at peace with all men. We are not to repay evil with evil or seek vengeance against our enemies. But rather, we are to "give them to eat and drink" if they are hungry and thirsty (Rom. 12:17-21). In Romans 13:1-14, we are instructed to honor authority, to walk in love by owing no man anything except love, to awake from our sleep, to cast off the works of darkness, to put on the armor of light, to walk honestly, to put on Messiah and to make no provision to fulfill the lusts of the flesh. These orders are tall orders to carry out but we must remember that by doing all of these things, we fulfill the law which finds its end in love.

In Titus 3:1-2, we are reminded of our citizenship and enlistment status and our responsibility to that status as we are directed to "...be subject to principalities and powers, to obey magistrates, to be ready to every good work, to speak evil of no man, to be no brawlers, but gentle, showing all meekness unto all men." And finally we are to walk worthy of God who has called us (Eph. 4:1).

The prophet Micah sums it up succinctly by stating that we are to "love mercy, to do justly, and to walk humbly before our God" (Mic. 6:8).

To complete a tour of duty, every good soldier must be conditioned and prepared for battle. He or she usually undergoes an intensive training period known as boot camp. It is here that the soldier is trained physically and prepared mentally for what lies ahead. In addition to the physical training, there is usually a lot of discussion about the enemy and what might be encountered on your tour of duty. This time is probably the most integral component of the military experience prior to engagement. A soldier must be a fit vessel.

Training in Haganah involved time being spent preparing for the battle, so to speak. At the beginning of class we slowly raise our heart rate and warm up by doing stretches, sit-ups, push-ups, shadow boxing, and various calisthenics to prepare our body and mind for the task at hand. These techniques are done in preparation to execute the maneuvers and military combatives that are the heart of this defense system. Just as it is important to train your body and your mind to be ready to counter an assault, it is just as vitally important to prepare yourself for spiritual warfare. Ultimately, we are told to present our bodies as a living sacrifice (Rom. 12:1). To that end, there are certain protocols, "spiritual warm ups" if you will, that are necessary to attend to prior to engaging in battle.

First and foremost, there is a need to allow the Spirit of God to shine His light into the depths of our hearts as we examine ourselves (Prov. 20:27, Ps. 15, Ps. 139:23-24) and as we confess our sins (1st John 1:9, Ps. 24:3-4, Ps. 51). Ephesians 4:23-32 tells us to be renewed in the spirit of our mind and to put on the new man. We are told to put away stealing, lying, anger, bitterness and corrupt communication (Eph. 4:29-32, Col. 3:8, 1st Pet. 2:1); our directive is to not give a place in our lives to Satan by doing these things. Moreover, we are called to be tender hearted, forgiving and kind to one another (Eph. 4:32) just as our Commander in Chief has been to us. It is only after this initial preparation that we are ready for the next level of engagement.

In Haganah, the warm up is the most important task. As we step onto the mat to do the warm up, we hear the instructor give an important directive. We hear him say, "Stay loose...life is good"! He was referring to our temporal life. But for the believer, life IS good because we know that we are His elect, that we are loved and that we have the privilege of operating in the fullness of the Kingdom principles. Yes, life IS good for those that know God in an intimate way. There is a big difference between head knowledge "know God" and heart knowledge "know God". Heart knowledge invokes an intimacy with God that head knowledge could never approach. The Bible invites everyone to "...taste and see that the Lord is good" (Ps. 34:8). As believers, we have to "stay loose" and let the love of God flow through us. We are called to show forth the goodness of the Lord as we walk in love (1st John 4:7-8, 1st John 4:15-21, John 15:10-11, John 13:34, Luke 6:27-32, Matt. 5:44). When asked about the greatest commandment, Jesus spoke about loving God with all of our souls, hearts, and minds and loving our neighbors as ourselves. He added that all the law hangs on these two commandments (Matt. 22:37-40). God's entire spiritual law can be summed up in this word love. The apostle Paul explained in

Romans 13:10 that "love is the fulfillment of the law". He also states that God's law is spiritual (Rom. 7:14) and that this law is fulfilled by spiritual love, agape love. Agape love is God's own love because scripture says that God is love (1st John 4:8). John 3:16 says that "God so loved (agape) the world that He gave His only begotten Son, that whoever believes in Him should not perish but have eternal life". Agape love is the fruit of the Spirit of God dwelling within us (Gal. 5:22). Agape love is characterized as being patient, kind, truthful, unselfish, trusting, believing, hopeful, and enduring (1st Cor. 13:4-13). Moreover, scripture says that "love is shed abroad in our hearts" (Rom. 5:5) by the Ruach Ha Kodesh (Hebrew Holy Spirit of God). We only know love because God first loved us (1st John 4:19). Scripture speaks a lot about the love walk that a believer is to maintain (John 13:34-35, 1st John 2:6, 2nd John 1:6, 1st Cor. 13:1-3).

Love is the supreme interpretation of Torah because love is the overriding principle that defines how all laws are to be obeyed. Surprisingly after Paul spends time in Romans and Galatians arguing against their need to observe Torah, he answers their question about how to "fulfill the law" by penning Romans 13:8-10: "Owe no man anything, but to love one another; for he that loves another hath fulfilled the law. For this, Thou shalt not commit adultery, Thou shalt not kill, Thou shalt not steal, Thou shalt not bear false witness, Thou shalt not covet; and if there be any other commandment, it is briefly comprehended in this saying, namely, Thou shalt love thy neighbor as thy self. Love works no ill to his neighbor; therefore, love is the fulfilling of the law." He restates this in Galatians 5:14: "For all the law is fulfilled in one word, even in this; Thou shalt love thy neighbor as thyself." The Kingdom of God is ruled by the law of love.

We are to be motivated by love (Jude 21), marked by love (1st Cor. 13:4-13), and mastered by love (1st Cor. 13:4-7) because love never fails and in the end, love fulfills the law (Rom. 13-10). The mark of a believer is not activity for God, it is love. The more we love, the "tastier" we are for others and then we can truly say, "taste and see that the Lord is good" (Ps. 34:8).

Love and commandment keeping are linked together. Notice the scriptures that remind us of this: 1st John 5:3 states, "For this is the love of God, that we keep His commandments". 2nd John 6 tells us that it is love to walk in His commandments. 1st John 2:4-5 states, "He who says, "I know Him", and does not keep His commandments, is a liar and the truth is not in him. But, whoever keeps His word, truly the love of God is perfected in him". And finally, "He who has my commandments and keeps them, it is he who loves Me" (John 14:21). "Love" is the way that God lives and it is the way He commands us to live. It is the halachah (Hebrew the way one walks). This halachah is what the apostle Paul had in mind when he wrote to "walk in the spirit" (Gal. 5:25). In telling us how to live, God gave us directives (teachings) to help us understand how to do that. He gave us His Torah, His teachings and instructions. In fact, Torah means teaching or instruction which is far from most believers' understanding of the meaning of that word. Proverbs 3:18 reminds us that, "She (Torah/wisdom) is a tree of life to all who take hold of her, and happy is everyone who retains her". The Law (as some call Torah) was never meant to be a burden but rather it was meant to be instructional, a teaching.

The word Torah is traditionally referring to the first five books of the Bible and includes the 10 commandments. It was given to Moses and the Israelites at Mount Sinai AFTER they were delivered out of Egyptian bondage. Torah was given to these now redeemed people to teach them now how to live a redeemed lifestyle moving forward. Likewise, after we are redeemed, we must come to a new and deeper understanding of the Torah as our instruction Manual.

From a Messianic perspective, we can see two major continuities in Torah beginning in Genesis. First is the theme of redemption. The human race, created in the image of God, has a destiny which will be fulfilled despite failure and opposition. Early in the story, when the sin of Adam and Eve seems to have sidetracked God's purpose, God promises a seed, an offspring of the woman who will defeat the opposition. The theme of the promised seed carries throughout the book.

Second is the theme of covenant. After the flood, God makes a covenant with the whole nation through Noah. Then, when God raises up a restored humanity through Abraham, He establishes a covenant with him as well, which God will preserve and pass on to each succeeding generation.

These themes of redemption and covenant are foundational to the whole Torah and to all the scriptures built upon it, the Manual, the Bible that we possess and read today. These themes will enable us to read Torah, not just as an ancient history or rulebook, but as a story of Creation to completion, a story filled with hope for our world. In this understanding, Creation is not an end in itself, but in moving to a goal — the completion of God's order and shalom (peace, wholeness). Indeed, this theme of Creation and its consummation underlies the entire Torah.

This theme also unlocks the meaning of our own lives. It defines our tour of duty. When God created humankind, He gave them a role in improving and maintaining His Creation: "Then God blessed them, and God said to them, "Be fruitful and multiply; fill the earth and subdue it; have dominion over the fish of the sea, the birds of the air, and over every living thing that moves on the earth" (Gen. 1:28). Humans are to fill the earth that God created and to subdue and rule it in a divine-human partnership. God put Adam and Eve in the Garden and told them to "keep it" (Gen. 2:15). This human tending and keeping of the Garden was to increase it until the whole earth becomes a Garden and Creation reaches the fulfillment for which it was designed. However, as we know, sin entered the picture to disrupt the plan and because of their disobedience, Adam and Eve were expelled from the Garden and were cut off from the Tree of Life.

Their exile sets the stage for the human quest throughout the rest of Torah, and into our own lives, the quest for the Tree of Life. Judaism sees Torah as the Tree of Life. When the Torah is held up before the congregation, the believers recite the part of Psalm 119 that tells us that Torah "is a Tree of Life to all who take hold of it". Cleaving to Torah, then, will open the way back to the Tree of Life.

In Matthew 5:17, we read the words of the Messiah regarding Torah. He says, "Think not that I am come to destroy the law or the prophets; I am not come to destroy but to fulfill." The word we read "law" is Torah in Hebrew and its main meaning is teaching or instruction rather than a legal regulation. When many well-meaning Christians read this they say that when Jesus (Hebrew Yeshua) "fulfilled the law", He brought it to an end. In the verses that followed this verse, we see that this isn't true. The key to understanding this verse is to use a Hebraic viewpoint of the phrase "to fulfill the law". This phrase is a rabbinic idiom which means to uphold or establish (Hebrew lekayem) as well as to complete or accomplish. In his book entitled, New Light on the Difficult Words of Jesus: Insight from His Jewish Context, David Bivin states, "...fulfill the law" is often used as an idiom to mean properly interpret the Torah so that people can obey it as God really intends." We must remember that Jesus (Hebrew Yeshua) never had a King James Bible; He had Torah and when He said, "It is written..." He was referring to Torah. Nowhere did Jesus ever disavow the Ten Commandments or any part of Torah. In fact, the Ten Commandments and much of Torah is reiterated throughout the New Testament. It has been said that the Old Covenant is the New Covenant concealed and the New Covenant is the Old Covenant revealed.

When Paul exhorts believers regarding "putting on the full counsel of the Lord" (Acts20:27), he is referring to the counsel and understanding found in Torah. The early church did not teach what is commonly taught in Christianity today. Believers in the first and second centuries were taught the Torah! After all, the Brit Hadasha (Hebrew New Covenant) is not really a new walk, it is a re-newed walk of Torah, fulfilled by the righteousness and sinless life of our Jewish Lord, Yeshua Ha Massiach (Hebrew Jesus, the Messiah). If we are believers and followers of Messiah then we are to walk as He did. He is our example.

The word Torah is derived from two other Hebrew words: "or" (Strong's #216) meaning "light" and "yarah" (Strong's #3384) which means to "shoot an arrow."

The "or" (light) of creation was God speaking into the darkness to bring light and order to the chaos. In the Hebrew, the account of the creation calls the environment "Tohu v' bohu" meaning "chaos and emptiness". Then, God said, "Light be" (Gen. 1:3). This "or", this primordial Light, existed before the creation of the sun; it was the Divine "Light" of God Himself that pierced the darkness and brought the order.

The second root word of Torah is "yarah" meaning to "shoot an arrow." We can connect this idea to an archer shooting an arrow. If the arrow misses the target for which it was intended, it is called "sin" which simply means to miss the mark. As the Word reminds us, "we have all sinned (missed the mark that God intended) and fallen short of the glory of God" (Rom. 3:23). In an interesting connection, Rabbi Messer says in his book, Torah: Law or Grace, that "when your confession (Jesus) matches your conduct (Torah), it is called Ha Kavod (Hebrew the Glory)." We hit the mark, so to speak, when we walk in His ways and follow His teachings, His Torah. Torah is the constitution of the Kingdom of God and it is what provides us our citizenship status and allows us to claim our rights under the blood of our Messiah, our Commander in Chief. We must read the "constitution" to know our rights as a citizen of the Kingdom so we can read it to the enemy when we are captured! The enemy cannot detain citizens of the Kingdom when they know their rights!

The ongoing battle of the ages is not necessarily to cast out demons but rather it is to stay rightly related to God. If we want to be rightly related to God, then we must be rightly related to Jesus and rightly related to the Manual, the Word of God. There is power and authority in His Word (2nd Tim. 3:16-17) and in His name. When we stay rightly related to God and walk the love walk that we are commanded to walk, we will war more effectively during our tour of duty. But, more importantly, WE BRING THE KINGDOM OF GOD TO EARTH.

The next "spiritual callisthenic" important in our training and execution of our duty is to spend time in thanksgiving, worship, and praise, (Ps. 92:1-2, Ps. 103:1-5, Ps. 149:1-6, Ps. 24:7-10.) The Scripture says to "come into His gates with thanksgiving and enter His courts with praise" (Ps. 100:4-5, Ps. 22:3). There is an interesting aside about verse 4 of Psalm 100. This verse has 4 out of the 7 Hebrew words used for thanks or thanks giving. The seven Hebrew words are todah, barak, tehilla, halal, yadah, zamar, and shabach. Psalm 100, verse 4 is the only place in the Bible that all of these words are present at one time. Each word has a slightly different meaning. Todah means a thanksgiving choir; barak means to kneel in thanksgiving; tehilla means to sing a song in thanksgiving; halal means to give thanks by being clamorously foolish; yadah means to give thanks with extended hands; zamar means to give thanks with a musical instrument; and shabach means to give thanks in a loud tone. So, the verse reads: "Come into His courts with thanksgiving (todah) and enter His courts with praise (tehilla); be thankful (yadah) onto Him, and bless His name (barak). Thus Psalm 100:4 would read, "Come into His courts with a thanksgiving choir and enter His courts singing a song of thanksgiving; give thanks to Him with extended hands and kneel in thanksgiving".

The book of Psalms is filled with words of thanksgiving and praises to God. For the believer, an attitude of thanksgiving is a practical orientation to a lifestyle of genuine appreciation for the acts of God in one's life. The writer of 1st Thessalonians 5:18 speaks words of instruction to us saying, "in everything give thanks: for this is the will of God in Messiah Jesus concerning you." Just what is this will of God? It is to thank Him in ALL things. We need to thank Him even in the midst of our battles. We need to thank Him for closed doors as well as opened doors. We need to thank Him for the things prayed for and not yet seen (Heb. 11:1, Eph. 5:20, Ps. 116:17, John 13:13-14.) We need to thank Him for the situations that we don't understand or can't make sense of, and yes, even for the gift of pain that's even harder to understand or accept. Thanksgiving causes a release in the supernatural. And, thanksgiving produces worship! So important is the aspect of thanksgiving, praise and worship that Jesus taught us the perfect model of approaching God the Father in the Lord's Prayer (Matt.6:9-13). It begins with praise and worship and then asks with assurance for daily sustenance, direction and protection. We can only end that prayer with an attitude of thanksgiving for these provisions. Also, we can be so thankful that He directs our footsteps (Ps. 37:23, Prov. 3:5-6, Prov. 16:9), that He guides us with His eye (Ps. 32:8) and that He gives us the desires of our heart as we delight ourselves in Him (Ps. 37:4). Moreover, His Word says that "no good thing will He withhold from those that walk uprightly" (Ps. 84:11).

In the scriptures, we see several references of Jesus giving thanks. He blessed and gave thanks for the loaves and fishes before feeding the multitude (John 6:11). He thanked the Father that He revealed things unto babes (Matt. 11:25). He gave thanks before He drank the cup of wine at His last Seder (meal) (Matt. 26:27). And He also thanked the Father that He heard His prayers (John 11:41).

The Word of God tells us that giving thanks is a good thing (Ps. 92:1) and that it is commanded of us (Ps. 50:14,

Phil. 4:6). And, we also know that we are in good company when we offer thanksgiving to God because all the heavenly host of angels and elders are engaged in it too (Rev. 4:9, Rev. 7:11, Rev. 11:16-17). Our acts of thanksgiving should be offered to God through Messiah (Col. 3:17, Heb. 13:15), and in the name of Messiah (Eph. 5:20). We should thank God publicly (Ps. 35:10) and privately (Dan. 6:10). We should thank Him in everything and for everything and always (1st Thess. 5:18, Eph. 1:16, Eph. 5:20, 1st Thess. 1:2, 2nd Corin. 9:11). In Nehemiah 12:31 and 12:40, we see that it is good to thank God upon completion of great undertakings. We are also to express thanksgiving before we eat (John 6:11, Acts 27:35). As we remember the goodness and mercy of God and reflect upon His holiness, we are to give thanks (Ps. 106:1, Ps. 107:1, Ps. 136: 1-3, Ps. 30:4, Ps. 97:12). We are to thank God for the gift of the Messiah and for His power and reign (2nd Cor. 9:15, Rev. 11:7). It is good to offer thanksgiving for deliverance through Messiah from our in-dwelling sin (Rom. 7:23-25) and for victory over death and the grave (1st Cor. 15:57). We can thank God for the nearness of His presence in our life and for our appointment to this commission, our tour of duty (Ps. 75:1, 1st Tim. 1:12). There were many who walked before us exemplifying thanksgiving in their lives: David (1st Chron. 29:13), the Levites (2nd Chron. 5:12-13), Daniel (Dan. 2:23), Jonah (Jon. 2:9), Simeon (Luke 2:28), Anna, (Luke 2:28), and Paul (Acts 28:15).

And finally, it is interesting to note that throughout the Torah, the Lord, Himself, commanded the Israelites to have the tribe of Judah always go out first in the battle. In Hebrew, Judah means, I will thank/praise the Lord. May we always first offer the sacrifice of praise as we fight the battles that are before us (Heb. 13:15). May we send out Judah first!

Psalm 103 gives us five specific things to be thankful for: God forgives all of our sins; He heals all of our diseases; He redeems our lives from destruction; He crowns us with loving kindness and tender mercies; and, He satisfies our mouths with good things so that our youth is renewed like the eagles. It is in this youth that we can war, and defeat the enemy by setting the captives free!

Chapter III

OUR
ADVERSARY

Our training in Haganah, taught us that gathering accurate combat intelligence on the enemy is crucial. In that venue, it might be a simple thing like observing a slight facial change or muscle twitch indicative of an impending attack. Therefore, we were taught to be acutely observant and to always be in an offensive mode and mind set.

Military strategists will tell you that learning the facts about your enemy is a critical factor in winning battles. In fact, one of the most important maxims of war is "Know your enemy", a maxim most often forgotten by believers. It is mandatory for us to understand who the enemy is, what the enemy does and how he does it. For the believer, this information is located in the Manual, the Word of God. We see in Ezekiel 28:12-19 an extensive description of our enemy Lucifer. He was God's angel of worship who because of his sins and his pride came to a fitting end as he was cast from the garden. His name is more commonly referred to as Satan (Hebrew Ha Satan) meaning adversary. He also is known by several other names such as the devil (Matt. 4:1), the evil one (John 17:15), the tempter (Matt. 4:3), Beelzebub (Matt. 12:24), Belial (2nd Cor. 6:15), the prince of this world (John 12:31), the ruler of the kingdom of the air (Eph. 2:2), the god of this age (2nd Cor. 4:4), the accuser of the brethren (Rev. 12:10), the father of lies (John 8:14), and the serpent and the dragon (Rev. 20:2), to name a few. All of these names reveal something about his character. It is in Ezekiel 28: 12-19 that we learn about his creation, his sin, and his fall.

Ezekiel 28:12-19 reads, "You were the seal of perfection, full of wisdom and perfect in beauty. You were in Eden, the garden of God; every precious stone adorned you: carnelian, chrysolite, and emerald, topaz, onyx and jasper, lapis, lazuli, turquoise and beryl. Your settings and mountings were made of gold; on the day you were created they were prepared. You were anointed as a guardian cherub, for so I ordained you. You were on the holy mount of God; you walked among the fiery stones."

"You were blameless in your ways from the day you were created till wickedness was found in you. Through your widespread trade you were filled with violence, and you sinned. So I drove you in disgrace from the mount of God, and I expelled you, guardian cherub, from among the fiery stones. Your heart became proud on account of your beauty, and you corrupted your wisdom because of your splendor."

"So I threw you to the earth; I made a spectacle of you before kings. By your sins and dishonest trade you have desecrated your sanctuaries. So I made fire come out from you, and it consumed you, and I reduced you to ashes on the ground in the sight of all who were watching. All the nations who knew you are appalled at you; you have come to a horrible end and will be no more."

This passage tells us that Lucifer walked in God's garden and enjoyed access to God only to find himself because of his sin to be stripped of all his glory and cast from God's presence. No wonder he hates us and seeks to destroy us. No wonder he seeks to separate us from our faith and rest in God by creating doubt, chaos and worry in our lives. The old saying in the world is misery loves company. Satan loves to make our lives miserable as he attempts to unseat our faith and rest in God's promises. He loves to distort the Word of God like he did with Eve (Gen. 3:1) when he asked her, "Yea, hath God said...?" At times, we can almost gauge our level of threat to Lucifer by the intensity of attacks toward us.

However, it isn't necessary to look for demonic activity behind every bush, but at the same time, we must be mindful of 1st Peter 5:8 that says, "Be sober minded; be watchful. Your adversary the devil prowls around like a roaring lion, seeking whom he may devour". John 8:44 defines Ha Satan, Satan, as follows: "He was a murderer from the beginning, and does not stand in the truth, because there is no truth in him."

Lucifer was created with stringed instruments and timbrels within him and he led worship in heaven before his fall (Ez. 28:13). Prior to his fall, Satan's greatest desire was to be king and to be worshipped. Since worship is love expressed, one of Satan's greatest desires even now is to steal our worship. He does that by creating doubt by speaking things to us that are contrary to the Word of God. If we doubt God then we have little reason to praise Him or worship Him. Isaiah 14:12-17 explains the many ways he wanted to exalt himself above God. It includes a long list of his desires for exaltation: "I will ascend into heaven..."; "I will exalt my throne..."; "I will sit upon the mount..."; "I will ascend above the heights..."; "I will be like the Most High God."

As he goes back and forth, day and night, accusing the brethren (1st Tim. 4:13, Rev. 12:10), he seeks to unseat us by attacking our thought life with his lies. He contends for our lives. His plan is to entrap us by deception and temptation. His intention is to steal our inheritance by challenging our very identity. That was the first thing Satan did when he tempted Jesus. He questioned His identity by saying, "IF you are the Son of God..." (Matt. 4:3). That's why it is vitally important for us to remember to Whom we belong...who we are in Messiah, and Who our Father is. If Satan can make us doubt who we are in Messiah, then he has inroads to the rest of our camp and our possessions. When he comes with his lies, we must remind ourselves of the Manual, the Word of God. The Word of God says:

I am God's child (John 1:12)	I am a minister of reconciliation for God (2 Cor. 5:17-21)
I am Messiah's friend (John 15:15)	I am God's co-worker (1 Cor. 3:9, 2 Cor. 6:1)
I am united with the Lord (1 Cor. 6:17-20)	I am seated with Messiah in heavenly realms (Eph. 2:6)
I am bought with a price (1 Cor. 12:27)	I am God's workmanship (Eph. 1:5)
I am a saint (set apart for God.) (Eph. 1:1)	I am confident that the good works God has begun in me will be perfected (Phil. 1:5)
I am complete in Messiah (Col. 2:10)	I have been justified (Romans 5:1)
I am free forever from condemnation (Rom. 8:1-2)	I have been adopted as God's child (Eph. 1:5)
I am assured all things work together for good (Rom. 8:28)	I have access to God through the Holy Spirit (Eph. 2:18)
I am free from any charge against me (Rom. 8:31-34)	I have been redeemed and forgiven (Col. 1:14)
I am established, anointed, sealed by God (2 Cor. 1:21-22)	I have been chosen and appointed to bear much fruit (John 15:16)
I am hidden with Messiah in God (Col. 3:3)	I may approach God with freedom and confidence (Eph. 3:12)
I am a citizen of Heaven. I am significant (Phil. 3:20)	I can do all things through Messiah who strengthens me (Phil. 4:13)
I am the salt of the earth (Matt. 5:13-14)	I cannot be separated from the love of God (Rom. 8:35-39)
I am the branch of the true vine, a channel of His life (John 15:1-5)	I belong to God – He is my Father.
I am a personal witness of Messiah (Acts 1:8)	I am God's temple (1 Cor. 3:16)

Another goal of his is to keep us distracted with the cares of this world so we cannot stay focused on what we are called to do. Frequently, he even keeps us engaged and entangled in "good" deeds and pursuits, knowing that good is the enemy of best. If you have done a good job but not the right job then it is a wrong job! Religion is Satan's greatest tool. If he can keep us playing church and not knowing about the Kingdom and Kingdom principles then he sidelines us and renders us ineffective in the battle. Sadly many Christian churches preach Jesus only and not about the Kingdom. It might be a hard word for many to hear but Jesus never preached Himself; He preached the gospel, the good news. Moreover, He never said to His followers, "Preach me"; He said preach the gospel, the good news. What is the good news? It is the good news about the Kingdom (Luke 4:43-44, Matt. 4:17, Matt. 24: 14)! Jesus is the door (John 10:9) to that Kingdom. We must understand the New Testament with a Hebraic mindset to comprehend the fullness of what is being said. In a Hebraic mindset, a door is an opening into another dimension. If we only tell people about the Door and not what's behind that Door in that other dimension then we have not told them the full truth. We must walk out a redemptive lifestyle by walking out the Kingdom principles. He is the Way (John 14:6) to God and to His Kingdom. The good news is not Jesus loves you even though He does! Jesus never preached Calvary because Calvary was not the good news! Yes, Jesus dying on Calvary was necessary to "buy back", to redeem the Kingdom which Adam lost at creation. But it even goes beyond that. He paid the price and provided the atonement for us to be citizens in His Kingdom! The only true gospel is the good news about the Kingdom of God. It is our job to preach this Kingdom and the Kingdom principles for living after salvation and in doing so we battle the very forces of evil. Luke 8:10 reminds us that "The knowledge of the secrets of the

Kingdom of God has been given to you". And, Yeshua (Jesus) Himself told his talmidim (Hebrew wise students, disciples) that He would give them the "...keys of the Kingdom of heaven..." (Matt. 16:13-19). The keys of the Kingdom of heaven are the laws, principles and statutes of God that must be adhered to by every citizen so that they may benefit from their citizenship rights and privileges in the Kingdom. We are "born again" into the Kingdom of God and must know and live by the laws of our Kingdom. It was in this same discussion that He spoke about binding and loosing on earth as it would be in heaven. Messiah had much to say about the Kingdom of God and the Kingdom mindset. See Luke 4:43-44, Matt. 4:17 and Matt. 24:14 for three of the many scriptures that speak to this. The apostle Paul did not only preach Jesus, he preached the Kingdom (Acts 28:30-31). In Matthew 25:34, we see that what we inherit is the Kingdom not Jesus. Not to minimize the work of Messiah, but we must know about the Kingdom as well as the King! So important was the Kingdom that it is understood to be the central message of Jesus (Hebrew Yeshua) Himself.

In wartime (the daily hindrances of life), there are many other traps of the enemy that can trip us up and serve to derail our love walk...offense is probably the biggest. Scripture says that offense will invariably come our way in life (Luke 17:1). When this happens, we must keep our accounts short with God, meaning forgive quickly so as not to give the enemy a foothold in our lives. Many of us who have been deeply wounded in battle are unable to function properly in our calling because of the wounds and hurts that offenses have caused in our lives. Most often, these wounds have been inflicted by "friendly fire", from those closest to us. In Psalm 55:12-14, David bemoans this very situation as he states, "For it is not an enemy who reproaches me;

then I could bear it. Nor is it one who hates me who has exalted himself against me; then I could hide from him. But it was you, a man my equal, my companion and my acquaintance. We took sweet counsel together, and walked to the house of God in the throng." Sometimes, the closer the individual is to us the more severe the offense. The truth is that only those you care about can hurt you. That is because, often, we have invested ourselves more and have higher expectations of people closest to us. Therefore, when there is a fall from grace, the fall is great! It is important to be prepared and armed for offenses because they surely come. Offense is one of Satan's greatest tools to take prisoners captive and to hold them hostage even for a lifetime. They are then forced to do Satan's will, often never realizing they are being held captive in his camp. This is because the offense is sometimes hidden by pride. It is our pride that stops us from admitting we have been wounded and from realizing the true condition of our heart. Pride can cause us to have a victims' mentality by which we justify our behavior by thinking, "I was mistreated and misjudged; therefore, I am justified in my response to the situation." Two wrongs never make a right!

In 2nd Timothy 2:24-26, the apostle Paul instructed his young charge in this manner: "And a servant of the Lord must not quarrel but be gentle to all, able to teach, patient, in humility correcting those who are in opposition, if God perhaps will grant them repentance, so that they may know the truth, and that they may come to their senses and escape the snare of the devil, having been taken captive by him to do his will." When we look at life through past hurts, and rejections, it can affect how we view God. We might say to ourselves, maybe He doesn't love me; how can He allow this to happen to me; I can't trust Him and therefore cannot believe Him or His promises. We end up doubting His goodness and faithfulness and cannot rely on the validity of His promises in our life because of the offenses. Instead, it is better to repent of unforgiveness and leave the rest to God because it is written that vengeance or repayment is the Lord's business (Rom. 12:19). Forgiveness is giving up our resentment against someone and our right to get even no matter what was done to us. With the help of God, we need to release our offenses quickly (Col. 3:13) to be an effective warrior.

The story of the Messiah's betrayal by Judas offers another interesting insight into the insidious nature of offense. In John 12:3-8, we are told that Mary used a pound of spikenard, a very costly ointment, to anoint the feet of the Messiah. Judas Iscariot was also present at that time according to the record. He objected to this apparent frivolous use of the oil and asked why it wasn't sold instead for three hundred pence (a year's wages) and given to the poor. His concern was not for the poor but rather to obtain the money for himself. He took offense to her adoration and act of worship. It was that spirit of offense that led to the ultimate betrayal of Messiah. Offense is insidious and opens the door for the enemy's work in our lives. It hinders our faith, our worship and our praise of our God, our Commander in Chief. It stops us from entering into His rest. Offenses and problems will try our patience and disrupt our rest. We only need to look at the story of Job to see an extreme example of this.

And finally, there are those times too that we must remind ourselves not to take offense with God because it is Him who engineers the circumstances in our lives---all of the circumstances. The test of our loyalty will always come at the very point of that understanding. Along that line, we only have to look at our Messiah to know that He Himself was tested in this very point. The Manual says in Matt. 4:4 that after He was immersed and acknowledged as God's Beloved Son, He was led by the Spirit into the wilderness to be tempted by Satan. As hard as it is to acknowledge this fact, it is often the Spirit of God who will arrange an attack. It was the Spirit of God that led Him into that wilderness experience. The Father allowed this in His life I believe to demonstrate for us how Yeshua (Jesus) used the Sword of the Spirit to defeat the enemy. We know that all scripture is God breathed and is given for doctrine, reproof, correction, and instruction in righteousness (2nd Tim. 3:16). By Messiah's example, we can know that when, not if, but when, He leads us into the wilderness, He will also lead us out! And, even sustain us while we walk through it. Romans 8:28 reminds all soldiers that all wilderness experiences will work together for their good because they are loved and are called according to His purpose. And, remember, every soldier will definitely walk through places called the wilderness during his or her tour of duty. This experience separates the men from the boys, so to speak and it is here in these wilderness experiences that we either continue our tour of duty or we turn back. Of course, this is a huge piece of the battle that is rarely discussed with new enlistees as it would be initially too overwhelming to even imagine having to endure such experiences. The wilderness experiences are never meant to defeat us or destroy us but rather to develop our character. Therefore, we must learn to worship God in these trying times of the war so that we can stay focused, be filled with His Spirit, and avoid being derailed by offense.

It is wise to remember that every temptation and offense carried out by Satan is an attempt to bring us out of faith and out of our belief and rest in God's Word and His promises for our life. When we have unbelief, it satisfies Satan by making God out to

THE WARRIOR'S HANDBOOK - A GUIDE TO SPIRITUAL SURVIVAL

be a liar; but Scripture tells us that God does not lie (Num. 23:19). Satan is the father of lies (John 8:44) and he continually attempts to plant seeds of doubt and lies against the Word of God in our minds. His greatest tool is the constant battering and wearing down of the soldiers of God. Think you are tough enough to fight this constant battering? Well, think again! Scientists from the United States Army Research Institute have found that even the most elite combat soldiers are not immune to the detrimental effects of stress. In several training exercises where elite Army officers were exposed to moderate levels of sleep deprivation alone, studies showed there were elevated cortisol levels, for one, which led to changes in mood, reduced vigor, increased fatigue, confusion and depression.

Battle fatigue gets the best of warriors! We must have our fellow soldiers' backs and cover them when they are under heavy enemy fire. We must lift them up on our shoulders when they are wounded and often we must carry them for miles and miles to get beyond the enemy fire. There are even times we must do immediate CPR to save their very life. It can all be enough to overwhelm even the most seasoned warrior. So, we must be vigilant to recognize battle fatigue and deal with it promptly as it will render us ineffective in this man's army. If we don't deal with it, we will become embittered soldiers who are consumed with our own physical and psychological wounds. And, because of the bitter sting we are left with from these wounds and battle scars, we will defile many. All we will be able to do at that point is to shrink back or recoil from the ugliness of others' wounds and gather in fox holes to talk about it. Or worse yet, when we have an encounter with such a fellow wounded soldier, we might even fire upon them as if they were the enemy. War can make you do crazy things. Be mindful.

It is incumbent upon us to know our Achilles heel and to bring it to the attention of the Commander in Chief who can apply the balm of Gilead to it. If we should sustain a serious battle wound — and we will, then we have to return to the base camp and do our first works of training to brush up on our skills once again. We also will need to rest in the Lord and frequently be still for long periods of time to allow total healing and to know that He is indeed God and He is in control even when we are not!

Chapter IV

ARMED AND DANGEROUS

In order to complete a tour of duty, a soldier must have the proper weapons at his or her disposal and must be well trained in their execution. In Haganah, we were trained both offensively and defensively. We trained in specific moves and combatives for use in close encounters with the enemy and we were well trained in the use of knives and guns. These tools were direct and effective when used properly. In addition, our metamorphosis into operatives included the psychological training and conditioning which was a major component of the offensive aspect of training.

Much like a Haganah operative, we, too, must have the proper weapons to use in this spiritual battle that is upon us. As we engage in this war, we have to rely on the weapons of warfare that are given to us by our Commander in Chief, the Messiah. But, unlike human weapons that can fail us, God has weapons that always ensure victory! We are armed and dangerous!!!

In Ephesians 6:10-17, we read about the defensive armor that God has given us to wear. But more importantly, in verse 17, we are told about a very important OFFENSIVE weapon! Our Commander in Chief has given us only ONE offensive weapon and because it is so powerful, one is all we need!

Our sole and greatest offensive weapon of warfare is the Sword of the Spirit, the Word of God (Eph. 6:17) and our faith in His Word. In the original Greek language, the meaning of the word sword in this verse is the same as dagger which is a weapon about 6 to 8 inches in length that was carried at the soldier's side. It is a precision weapon meant to be used in close, hand to hand combat. The dagger, as an offensive weapon, is meant to do physical and mental injury to another. Also in verse 17 we understand the translation in the original Greek language for WORD of God to be rhema which means sayings of God. The written Word of God is the logos, but in this verse we are given another definition for Word, rhema...the Living Word. The Bible is an armory of lethal heavenly weapons. It is where all the daggers are stored. Essentially we see that the sayings of God are the daggers we are to use to defeat the enemy. Jesus (Hebrew Yeshua) Himself used this weapon to defeat Satan! He said, "It is written..." as He recited Torah to Satan, specifically the words found in Deuteronomy. We are to walk after His example in all areas to be an effective warrior. We are reminded that "...the weapons of our warfare are not carnal, but mighty through God to the pulling down of strongholds..." (2nd Cor. 10:4). With His Word, we are able to accomplish our general assignment as well as our personal tour of duty. We are told in 1st Timothy 6:12 to "...fight the good fight of faith, lay hold of eternal life..." We need not concentrate on fighting the powers of darkness but rather we must continue to fight the good fight of FAITH! As we hear the Word of God, our faith is awakened. Romans 10:17 states, "So then faith comes by hearing and hearing by the Word of God". We are told in 2nd Timothy 2:15 "study to show thyself approved unto God, a workman that needs not be ashamed, rightly dividing the Word of truth." Hebrews 4:12 is a most militant statement about the Word of God. It says, "For the Word of God is living and powerful, and sharper than any two edged sword, piercing even to the division of soul and spirit, and of joints and marrow, and is a discerner of the thoughts and intents of the heart". We must learn to wield this Sword of the Spirit with precision and we can only do that by hearing, studying, and properly executing the Word of God.

There are other defensive weapons discussed in Ephesians 6:10-17 which are meant to protect us against the enemy. By the inspiration of God, the apostle Paul reminds us to put on the WHOLE armor to withstand the "...wiles of the devil", the constant battering. He tells us that our battle is against principalities and rulers of darkness in high places. We are told to stand when all else fails but we are to stand with our "...loins girt about with truth and having on the breastplate of righteousness". I think that the apostle Paul mentions this very important piece of armor first because we are told to "...guard your heart with all diligence because out of it flows the issues of life" (Prov. 4:23). Obviously if we are mortally wounded deep in our hearts with offenses and tribulations, we are like a sitting duck for the enemy and are vulnerable for attack. After that we are told to have on the gospel of peace, the shield of faith, and the helmet of salvation. We are to keep our armor on and the Word of God in our mouths continually so we give no place to the enemy. We have impressive defensive armor at our disposal, armor that is essential for our survival.

Having all of the armor helps us and protects us but having the correct mind set is mandatory to accomplish our tour of duty here. In Haganah, we were molded and psychologically groomed to be on the offense and that perspective has proven to be militarily the most valid and effective vantage point in battle. That is the vantage point from which we must continually fight in this present day spiritual battle. It is also important to remember that God has given us, through Yeshua (Hebrew Jesus), authority over the works of the enemy (1st John 3:8) and that because the Father has put all things under the Messiah's feet (Eph. 1:22), as we abide in Him, the enemy is under our feet as well (Luke 10:19). "Through God we will do valiantly, for it is He who shall tread down our enemies" (Ps. 60:12, Ps. 108:13). From a vantage point of being seated with God in heavenly places through Messiah Yeshua (Eph. 2:6), we are well positioned to identify and overcome the enemy. Psalm 91:14-16, tells us that God will deliver us, set us on high, answer us, be with us in trouble, deliver and honor us and satisfy us with a long life. These are powerful promises from a powerful God. It is in the Manual that we are reminded to be sober minded and vigilant because, "The night is far spent, the day is at hand: let us therefore cast off the works of darkness, and let us put on the armor of light" (Rom. 13:12).

For believers, intercession is a critical part of the psychological armamentarium necessary to sustain them. It is a behind the scenes, lethal weapon that the enemy cannot hack, penetrate or disarm. It serves to undergird the psychological stance of the believer and accomplishes the secret mission given to these Special Ops individuals who are called to this task. This particular mission rarely incites public accolades, recognition or awards because it flies under the enemy radar and goes unnoticed. There is no snare or danger of infatuation or pride in intercession. It is a covert operation that brings forth results whereby the Commander is glorified. Although this covert operation is open to all enlistees, only a select few carry out this task as their full time assignment.

During war time, every soldier needs a bunker! A bunker is a place to take cover and regroup. In fighting our daily battles, just knowing that there is a special bunker in which to take rest and refuge is comforting. So, in the midst of this war, we have to remember that we have El Elyon (Hebrew Most High God) as our Commander in Chief, our resting place. In Psalm 91:1-16, we are given instructions about our very special and necessary place of rest, our "bunker".

A look into this Psalm provides us with anti-terror, anti-murder, anti-fear, and anti-death truths that we will need to arm ourselves with for this war. It is important that this Psalm be the battle cry on our lips as we go into battle and until we finish our tour of duty and cross over into our promised homeland, a place not built with human hands (2nd Cor.5:1).

The first four verses of this Psalm talk about dwelling in the secret place of this Most High God (Hebrew El Elyon). But, we must choose to dwell there to enjoy the intimate covering and relationship with our Commander in Chief. To dwell in this secret place implies closeness, trust, and a personal relationship and respect of the Lord (see Ps. 15:1, Ps. 27:4, Ps. 37:3). Then, it says we will abide under the shadow of El Shaddai, Hebrew for Almighty God. Shaddai primarily means breasted (shad is breast in Hebrew). It indicates that God is the all bountiful and all nurturing provider. Next the Psalmist tells us that God is also our refuge (Ps. 91:2). Refuge in Hebrew indicates a shelter implying a place of hope and trust. In Psalm 91, we have a picture of the security and safety that can be found as we dwell in that secret place with our God. It is here in our bunker that we find our rest and solace in the heat of the battle. He is our hiding place and our ever present help in time of trouble (Ps. 46:1).

Another sure and powerful weapon of war that drives the enemy away and brings us into the very presence of God is our worship. We find that there in His presence is fullness of joy (Ps. 16:11)! The psalmist, David, gave Saul peace and respite from the evil spirits that tormented him with his melodies of worship to God. Satan hates to hear our worship and will do anything to bring distraction and discord to us to hinder our worship. Worship is our key to enduring in this war. Worship is a statement of our commitment to the Commander in Chief. It is our love expressed to our Commander even when we often don't understand the whole game plan of the war or our specific tour of duty. His thoughts and ways are never like our thoughts and ways (Is. 55:8-9)! But, we must remember that we are soldiers in HIS army doing our small but significant part in fulfilling HIS ultimate plan of Tikun Ha Olam...healing the world by walking out the Kingdom principles on this earth.

Our worship is the fast track for entering into the very throne room of God and we join with armies of angelic hosts (Rev. 4:9, Rev. 7:11, Rev. 11:16-17) as we worship God in the beauty of His holiness (Ps. 29:2).

And finally last, but certainly not least, is the weapon of controlling our thought life so as to give no place to the enemy. When we control our thought life, we control attitudes and subsequent behaviors; we conquer ourselves by conquering our mindset and Satan is not given any inroad in our lives. Change must come from the inside out and not the other way around. So, it is necessary to wash in the Word daily to renew our minds both to begin and to maintain that change.

We are called to die daily and to crucify our flesh (Rom. 8, Gal. 5) but we know that it is not speaking about a physical death. Crucifying your flesh is about changing your way of thinking so it aligns with the Word of God. So, being in the flesh is not an action but rather a way of thinking that opposes the Word of God. Your flesh is more than an external covering; it is a way of thinking. Your thought life is where Satan deposits his seeds of destruction. For example, people may say about a particular person, "that person was caught in adultery; they were really in the flesh". But, the truth of the matter is that they were "in the flesh" way before the act took place. People are "in the flesh" long before they commit adultery or covet, or lie, or are jealous. Those actions are only byproducts of fleshly thinking. Wrong thinking is a seed that has a harvest of failure. When we change our thinking to align with what the Word says, we change our actions. In John 6:63, we read that the Words of God are Spirit and that they are Life. It is said that right believing leads to right living. Proverbs 23:7 says that as a man thinks in his heart, so is he. Galatians 5 reminds us that our spirit and our flesh are always opposed to each other thus often making it difficult to do the right thing. This specific battlefield is where some of the most intense battles are fought.

We see the manifestation of this in our lives moment by moment. For example, we read that by His stripes we are healed and yet we often say to ourselves contradictory things like, "I will never feel good again". Where do these words of destruction come from? It comes from our flesh that's where! It is this flesh that must be crucified! We must walk by faith and not by sight because circumstances will often create F.E.A.R., *False Evidence Appearing Real.* We must take control of our thought life and constantly be looking for and expecting the enemy's ambush on this particular battlefield. We must not only hold our position but we must advance forward to take back (Matt. 11:12) what the enemy has stolen, much like David did at Ziklag (1st Sam. 30). As we advance, we gain new territory for the Lord as we set the captives free (Is. 61:1) and His will is done on earth as it is in heaven (Matt. 11:12). The Kingdom of God is brought to earth.

Chapter V

THE BENEFITS OF ENLISTMENT

When you enlist in any branch of the service, the contract you sign carries with it various benefits for enlisting. So it is with us, the ones who enlisted by saying yes to the call of God. We have a list of benefits that are available to us as well. Just as physical fathers provide many benefits, so our heavenly Father as our Commander in Chief also provides a number of spiritual benefits. As His soldiers, we can have fellowship with (1st John 1:3), access to (vv.9, 32), guidance by (Ps. 119:9, 2nd Tim. 3:17), protection by (John 10:29), and an inheritance from (Rom. 8:17) the Father.

In this war, we are always engaged on two fronts, two theaters of war simultaneously. We fight the enemy, tread on serpents and set captives free on one front while at the same time we wage the war of the inner man on the other front. The war of the inner man, however, is the ultimate battle that brings us closer to the realization of the greatest benefit of our enlistment. That benefit is our "shalom" which encompasses not only our peace, but also our wholeness and our healing- our total restoration, and our very destiny designed by God. God is our Jehovah Rophe, our Healer! He is a God of restoration (Deut. 30:3-16, Joel 2:25-26) but we must DECLARE RESTORE (Is. 42:22)! He promises us life instead of death and He promises that He will restore to us the years that the locust have eaten away. Our destiny is in His hands and no enemy in hell can thwart His plans as long as we continually say yes to Him (Job 42:2, Is. 14:27).

There are numerous other scriptures in our Manual that address the benefit of healing and restoration. Our Manual, the Bible, speaks not only about spiritual and emotional restoration but also about the things that pertain to our lives such as relationships, hope, health, faith, finances and our joy and honor. In Jeremiah 30:17, we are told that God will restore our health and will heal our wounds. Psalm 147:3 tells us that He comes to heal the brokenhearted. Isaiah 61:17 reminds us that He will give us a double portion instead of our shame and that we will have everlasting joy. We see that God restored Job's fortunes and even doubled them in Job 42:10, and Jeremiah 29:10-15 tells us that He has great plans for each one of us. Both Isaiah 1:18 and 2nd Corinthians 5:17 tell us about our spiritual restoration. In Psalm 51, we find that God creates a clean heart in us and that He restores us with the joy of His salvation. We learn about the God of hope in Romans 15:13 and Zechariah 9:12 even calls us "prisoners of hope" and tells us that we will be restored twice as much. Jeremiah 17:14 and Hosea 6:1 speak to our healing. When we follow His directives to be kind to one another, forgiving and merciful, and tenderhearted and compassionate, we are assured that God will bring restoration to our relationships in life (Eph. 4:32, Luke 6:36, Col. 3:12-14, 1st Pet. 4:8, Prov. 17:9, Matt. 18:15, Luke 15). This is especially so as we continue to walk the way of peace with all men as we are told to in Romans 12:14-18. The enemy comes to steal and rob from us and destroy us, but our Commander in Chief promises us that He defeats the enemy and that He gives us life and life more abundantly (John 10:10). All we have to do is seek His Kingdom first and all of these things will be added unto us (Matt. 6:33); but there is no guarantee that it will be added without a fight! The enemy of our souls fights us continually up to the day we cross over into our Promised Land.

Because of this, unfortunately, there is no magic waving wand that makes all of these benefits happen in our lives instantaneously. The deep intimacy and realization of these revelations is a process that is wrought with dirt and sweat in the trenches of the battlefield and more often than not, it is wrought in the wilderness experiences.

If you are in His service, the Spirit of God arranges these wilderness experiences. But, we must remember that when God arranges them, then God will use it for our ultimate good (Rom. 8:28) and if He led us into the wilderness, He will lead us out!

We know that the footsteps of a righteous man are directed by the Lord (Ps. 37:23) and that footsteps speak to the notion of process. When a blessing or the unfolding of our destiny is granted too soon, it is often not a blessing at all. A look at the story of the prodigal son (Luke 15:11-32) gives us an understanding of that very fact. In an effort to circumvent the process, the prodigal son asked for his inheritance before it's time and as we see, before he was ready for it because in his folly, he squandered it. He was not ready for what was handed to him. It proved to be his undoing. Similarly, if we circumvent the process, it could be our undoing. The process to our destiny and our blessing is to be unfolded one step at a time in our lives (Prov.4:12) and it cannot be hastened. Our benefits, blessings, and destiny are already there for us but we have to be readied for them. Usually we are where we are because God has ordained the process of that preparation. We are there by His design. Even Jesus went through the process in the human sense. After His immersion by John, Jesus was led by the Spirit into the wilderness to be tempted by the enemy. God orchestrated the test, most likely for our benefit, because what occurred was the Commander in Chief's greatest demonstration of how to defeat the enemy with the Word. Jeremiah 29:4-6 tells us that God allowed the people to be carried away into captivity but He blessed them while they were there. Again, He orchestrated the test. The children of Israel were in the desert for 40 years to humble them and to test their hearts (Deut. 8:2-3) and their shoes did not wear out. He orchestrated the test! God's agenda is always at work! We are told to let patience have her perfect work (James 1:4-8) because the trials so often used to develop our patience and our character ultimately yield the peaceable fruit of righteousness (Heb. 12:11). It is in this process that God perfects us as elite combat soldiers fit for His use.

Some of the character building that God instills in us through the adversities, trials, and battles we go through is only understood in retrospect; because, as we all have come to learn, His ways and thoughts are far above our understanding (Is. 55:8-9). We all know how stressful and even painful boot camp and service on the battlefield can be. And even the Manual reminds us, "now no chastening (discipline) for the present moment seemeth to be joyous, but grievous: nevertheless afterward it yieldeth the peaceable fruit of righteousness unto them which are exercised thereby" (Rom. 12:11). Not one soldier escapes this "exercise" because we have all suffered the aches and pains of boot camp and of our wilderness experiences. When we once again read the fine print of our contract of enlistment, we see that it says that the race is not always given to the swift or the battle to the strong (Eccl. 9:11). It is all about the process and during our tour of duty we are sure to learn that the process always works to our benefit (Rom. 8:28) no matter how painful. The victory goes to those who endure till the end! We see this in Revelation 15:1-3 where the victors sing the song of Moses and the song of the Lamb as their battle anthem!

But why must we endure this process? What is to be gained by it all? How do I make sense of it all when it hurts so badly? Just what is it that God is after in my life? What's the purpose? These are relevant, expected, and necessary questions that every soldier ponders in the quiet moments in his foxhole. Let's explore some of the possible answers to these questions because there are a number of things that God does in us and through us during these battles.

God's ultimate agenda for us is first and foremost our transformation into His image and glory (2nd Cor. 3:18, Eph. 1:1-14, Prov. 4:18). Battles are for our sanctification and they are used to transform us into the likeness of His Son in character and in spirit to reflect the glory of God (2nd Cor. 3:18). And, these battles will continue for the duration of our tour of duty (Phil. 1:6). Even though you feel at times that you will never complete this training and that the enemy is wounding you at every encounter, know that God has your back! You WILL prevail (2nd Cor. 3:17)! In fact, God sometimes allows these trials just to show us who He is and how He can help us through the battles.

Often God will use trials and tribulations as disciplinary measures because of our willful sins (Heb. 12:5-11). He is always looking for our obedience as it is more precious to Him than our sacrifices (1st Sam. 15:22). And much like a diamond that is formed under great pressure deep in the earth, we too are molded to be who He created us to be as He increases the process and the weight of the burdens. He then measures our growth by our response to the trials. In certain moments of great pressure He is usually removing our proclivity to be somebody we weren't meant to be. God can only get the glory when all of our preconceived notions and plans are dead and buried. The greatest example for us of ultimate submission to this death is seen when we read about our Commander in Chief in the Garden of Gethsemane. He prayed through His process with great drops of sweat and blood (Luke 22:44) as He prepared to give the ultimate sacrifice that would set the captives free. Sometimes we have to pray through our wilderness experiences and seek His face to find the God of our tight places, our Gethsemane because God wants us to see His power in our battles.

The worst wilderness battle we endure is usually the last place of victory before we cross over the Jordan into the promised land of our destiny and our purpose. But even then, God will continue preparing us for greater things much like he did with Joshua and the children of Israel at Gilgal (Josh. 4:19 – 5:12). Some say that Gilgal means circle of standing stones or that the place was called Gibeath Haaraloth which means hill of foreskins but the narrative goes on to tell us that the place was named Gilgal in memory of the reproach of Egypt being removed by the act of circumcision. Much like the circle of their flesh that was cut away, God often cuts away things from our lives to prepare us for what is next. He will cut away what is standing between us and our true destiny. Usually when He cuts something out of our lives, it is a sign that what He has ahead is bigger than what He cut away. When we have been in the Gilgal wilderness, we have to rest and heal like they did because after they were healed, they tasted the fruit of the Promised Land! And, likewise, we will too!

Another answer to the questions about the process is that He will put us through particular wilderness training events to test our faith and to build it up. We have to go back to the Manual to understand what it says about this aspect of training because most of the wilderness experiences are meant not only to transform us, but to teach us to trust Him. We will be able to say like Job, "Though He slay me, yet will I trust Him" (Job 13:15). In 1st Peter 1:6-7, we learn that we are to rejoice in this season of testing in fire because the trial of our faith is more precious than gold that perishes. We are also to rejoice in these trials because they produce patience and develop character in us (James 1:2-4). Paul reminds us in 2nd Corinthians 4:8-12 that we are troubled on every side and that we are distressed, perplexed, persecuted, and cast down but that we are NOT forsaken or destroyed! Death works in us to bring life to others. And, ultimately, our light afflictions, as Paul calls them, are working a far more exceeding and eternal weight of glory for us (2nd Cor. 4:16-18).

In John 15:1-2, we find that God often allows pruning in our lives to maximize our potential for service in His Kingdom. Often we are brought to our knees in submission as He teaches us about continual dependence on His grace and goodness. The apostle Paul, after praying 3 times to have his "thorn in the flesh" removed, finally states, "And He said unto me, My grace is sufficient for thee: for My strength is made perfect in weakness..." (2nd Cor. 12:9-11). In Hebrews 12:9-11 and Phil. 3:8-10, we are told that we share in Messiah's holiness and in His sufferings through tribulation and chastening and that we are taught perseverance as we develop character (Rom. 5:1-5).

We have to maintain a healthy theology of suffering in order to understand these things from God's perspective because most of the time when we are in the midst of the heat of the battle, things make little sense to us. We only need to look at the life of Joseph to understand situations like this. He loved God and he seemed to be doing the "right" thing and yet he ended up in a pit and was sold into slavery at the hands of his brothers. His process and testing were quite lengthy and involved so I am sure there were times that he might have been discouraged and wondered where God was in all of his tribulations; but, he had many tests to pass before he finally stepped into what God had for him. Much like Joseph's tests, every test we are faced with has to do with stewardship. Each test draws into question how we will steward our behavior, our resources, and our body while enduring the process. Events in Joseph's life serve to exemplify the fact that God can bring His shalom (Hebrew peace, prosperity, the absence of discord) out of what seemed to be an unlikely and an impossible situation. In Joseph's explanation to his brothers, we find his inspiration, "But as for you, ye thought evil against me; but God meant it unto good, to bring to pass, as it is this day, to save much people alive" (Gen. 50:20). It may have taken years to work out the details of going from the pit to the prison to the palace, but Joseph's life events were just part of the process to bring him to his ultimate purpose and destiny. We must remember that God's agenda is always at work through the suffering and we will come out stronger in the end!

Just as Joseph waited a long time to see the fullness of God's hand, so did David. Over a period of 14 years David fled from Saul and learned about waiting on God and His timing! The psalms that he wrote reflected his thoughts and prayers about his period of waiting. In Psalm 25:1-3, he prayed that as he trusted in God during his time of testing that he would not be ashamed. Romans 12:11 also tells us that as we wait and put our trust in God, we will not be ashamed. Psalm 27:11-14 still finds David in the midst of his enemies and waiting on God. He encourages and instructs himself in Psalm 37:7-9 by saying, "Rest in the Lord, and wait patiently for Him: fret not thyself because of him who prospereth in his way, because of the man who bringeth wicked devices to pass. Cease from anger, and forsake wrath: fret not thyself in any wise to do evil. For evildoers shall be cut off but those that wait upon the Lord, they shall inherit the earth". David tells us in Psalm 40:1 that when he waited patiently for the Lord, He inclined His ear to him and He heard his cry. Waiting is not a passive activity to be endured. Rather, it is a very dynamic activity! Psalm 40:31 reads, "But they that wait upon the Lord shall renew their strength; they shall mount up with wings as eagles; they shall run, and not be weary; they shall walk, and not faint". To better understand this verse, it is good to look at the original Hebrew word that is used for the word wait. It is qavah which means to bind together a cord by twisting. So to wait on the Lord, means to be twisted in with Him! How do we do that? We do that by reading and declaring His Word in our lives during our wilderness experiences of pain, confusion and waiting! During our battles, we have to hope in His Word as we are instructed to do in Psalm 119:74, 81.

It is during those times of intense pain, confusion, and waiting that we need to pray like David prayed with expectation when he said, "I had fainted, unless I had believed to see the goodness of the Lord in the land of the living" (Ps. 27:13). We must also remember that we are engraved on His palm; He will never leave us nor forsake us (Is. 49:16, Deut. 31:6); and HE IS A FAITHFUL GOD WHO KEEPS HIS PROMISES (Deut. 7:9)!!!

Your job, if you choose to accept it, is to be counted among this elite fighting force that sets the captives free! May He train your hands for war (Ps. 144:1)!

CPSIA information can be obtained
at www.ICGtesting.com
Printed in the USA
FFOW01n1025070916
27449FF